THE CYNICS VADE MECUM

Brian Boughton

...
Fitz Roy Publications 2001
...

First published in April 2001
By Fitzroy Publications
49 South Ford Road
Dartmouth
DevonTQ6
9QT

© 2001 Brian Boughton

ISBN 0-9540019-0-7

British Library Cataloguing in Publication Data
A CIP record of this book is available
From the British Library

Distributed by Fitz Roy Publications
Tel 01803 833 725

Brian Boughton's right to be identified as the author
of this book has been asserted by him in accordance with
the Copyright, Designs and Patents Act 1988

All rights reserved. No part of this book may be
reproduced by any means electronic or mechanical,
including photocopy or any information storage or retrieval
system without permission in writing from the publisher

Cover cartoon: Diogenes of Sinope
Cover design: Image Workshop, Totnes, Devon

Every effort has been made to trace copyright holders
and obtain permission. Any omission brought to
our attention will be remedied in future editions

Printed by Antony Rowe Ltd
Chippenham, Wiltshire

To Elizabeth, Emma & Peter

There is absolutely no evidence

that life was meant to be serious

Contents

Happiness	5
Leisure	7
Alcohol	9
Friends & Enemies	11
Anger	14
Ambition	15
Success	17
Work	20
Power	24
Leadership	25
Despots	27
War & Peace	29
Politics	32
Civil Service	36
Democracy	38
Public opinion	39
Liberty	40
Public speaking	41
Writing	44
Love	48
Women & men	51
Marriage	56
Sex	59
Nations	62
Social Classes	70
Time	72
Ages of Man	76
Death	80
The Future	82
Money	85
Poverty	91
Honesty	91
Truth	95
Knowledge	98
Education	109
Insanity	114
Religion	117

Preface

Aphorisms are wise sayings about the most interesting themes in life. They originate from many cultures, and can often be traced back to antiquity. Their appeal is therefore universal and enduring, and when good aphorisms distil truth into just a few words, they are also very beautiful. Sometimes they contradict each other, but then they are simply different facets of the same truth. Sometimes aphorisms from another age express values that are now outdated or outrageous. But these tell us about the authors or the age in which they lived, and when readers encounter such examples, they should reflect and smile, and not fume in moral indignation.

Aphorisms are often attributed to the great and the good, and can offer insights into their lives. Thomas Macaulay, Mark Twain, Churchill, Wilde and Quentin Crisp to name a few, used aphorisms in their conversation and writing. Some of their sayings were original but most were not, and as a result, reliable attribution is fraught with difficulty. One might apologise to the ancient Greek or Roman whose words have been wrongly attributed to a modern plagiarist, were it not for the fact that the Greeks and Romans were plagiarists themselves. I have given attributions to real life characters or their fictional mouthpieces depending on which seemed more interesting, and a few examples I have edited for the sake of brevity.

The aphorisms in this collection were gleaned from diverse sources, from after dinner speeches or magazines in dentists' waiting rooms, or from broadcasts on the car radio. For obvious reasons such records can be inaccurate, and if this is so, I ask the reader's forbearance. Our wealth of aphorisms expands continuously, and I have tried to use examples not previously published in an anthology.

This book is not a scholarly collection of quotations from Shakespeare or Confucius, for which the reader is referred elsewhere. Diogenes of Sinope and the other cynics of ancient Greece barked publicly about the follies and injustices of their world, and the name cynic means dog like or canine. Their new philosophy was intended to guide men to more thoughtful, happier lives, and in this spirit, I hope the Cynics Vade Mecum provides some insight into our own curious world.

Happiness

We feel happy when deep in the brain, 12 special nerve cells pulsate
Such is the contentment that all men seek
Unknown

•••

A man may know what he wants,
but he cannot choose what he likes
Unknown

•••

Being unable to cure death, wretchedness and ignorance,
men have decided instead to be happy
Blaise Pascal

•••

Happiness is good for the body
but grief develops the mind
Marcel Proust

•••

Life is full of loneliness, misery and poverty,
and it's all over too quickly
Woody Allen

•••

If you want peace of mind,
resign as general manager of the universe
Larry Eisenberg

•••

There is no pleasure in having nothing to do.
The fun is having lots to do and not doing anything
Mary Little

•••

Blessed is the person who is too busy to worry by day
and too sleepy to worry at night
Leo Aikman

•••

The secret about being miserable is not having the time to bother
George Bernard Shaw

•••

It is all very well to play with fools,
but these must be changed often,
or the entertainment becomes tiresome
Jean Paul Sartre

•••

Perfection is all that matters,
and I would transport all the riff raff
from Bristol to Botany Bay
to save one beautiful woman a single headache
Sir Humphrey Penhalligan

•••

Life would be happier if we were born aged eighty
and gradually approached eighteen
Mark Twain

•••

If I had my life over again,
I'd make the same mistakes, only sooner
Unknown

•••

It takes four adults to take one child to the circus
Bertram Mills

•••

Better to forgive and smile,
than to remember and be sad
Rossetti

•••

Anything can be funny as long
as it happens to somebody else
Will Rogers

•••

Happiness is more liking what you have
and less getting what you want
Quentin Crisp

•••

I am happy here, it's a wonderful place,
especially as I have no choice
Buddhist

•••

To some extent I lived in the future,
a habit which is the death of happiness
Quentin Crisp

...

If you want your dreams to come true you must wake up
Unknown

...

Its pretty hard to tell what brings happiness;
poverty and wealth have both failed
K *Hubbard*

...

Everything is disappointing in practice
Unknown

...

When my usband and I retire,
I ope to find a penis
Mme Yvonne De Gaulle

...

There is absolutely no evidence to suggest
that life was meant to be serious
Unknown

...

Leisure

When you are overtaken by the urge to exercise,
lie down until the feeling passes off
Thurber

...

If the TV and the refrigerator were not so far apart,
some people would get no exercise
Unknown

...

The only exercise some people get is jumping to conclusions,
running down friends, sidestepping responsibility
and pushing their luck
Unknown

...

The trick about successful walking is knowing when to stop
Bill Bryson

...

Waltz faster dear, this is a quickstep
Unknown

...

If you play bad music people don't listen,
and if you play good music they don't talk
Oscar Wilde

...

Art is the only serious thing in the world,
and the artist is the only person who is never serious
Oscar Wilde

...

You never appreciate the beauty of the world until you try to paint it
Unknown

...

Chess is too difficult for a game and not serious enough for a science
Napoleon Bonaparte

...

Golf without bunkers or hazards would be monotonous,
and so would life
B C Forbes

...

The more I practice golf, the luckier I get
Jack Nicklaus

...

There are three things to avoid on a sailing boat, a step ladder,
a wheelbarrow and any member of the Royal Navy
Unknown

...

The main difference between Rugby League and Rugby Union
is the former get their hangovers on Mondays
Tom Dand

...

The only difference between professionals and amateurs
is that one is paid by cheque and the other in cash
Harvey Smith

...

It would astound mountaineers to know
that most of us avoid mountains because they are there
S Barker

...

Alcohol

Let your boat of life be light, with enough to eat and enough to wear
And a little more than enough to drink,
for thirst is a dangerous thing
Jerome K Jerome

...

There is nothing yet contrived to produce more pleasure
than a good tavern
Dr Johnson

...

The best part of a good meal is not what you eat
but who you eat with and the wine you drink
Unknown

...

Whisky is a torchlight procession that marches down the throat
Unknown

...

Too much wine will dull a man's desire,
and indeed it will in a dull man
Tom Jones

...

Wine is only sweet to happy men
Unknown

...

I have taken more out of alcohol
than alcohol has taken out of me
Churchill

...

You can't drink all day
unless you start in the morning
Unknown

...

Too much good whisky is barely enough
Ronald Reagan

•••

Work is the curse of the drinking classes
Unknown

•••

If you drink enough whisky
you won't catch worms
Unknown

•••

The Scots can barely stay off the booze long enough
to take their driving tests
Duke of Edinburgh

•••

When Republicans poisoned the Dublin water supply,
the only survivors were a couple of drunks
Unknown

•••

An Irish queer is one who prefers women to booze
Unknown

•••

A drunk says what a sober person thinks
Unknown

•••

The ancient Persians always debated things twice,
once when they were drunk and again when they were sober
C S Lewis

•••

Good writers are drinking writers
and drinking writers are good writers
Ernest Hemingway

•••

Reality is an Irish notion brought on by lack of alcohol
Unknown

•••

There are 150 words in Arabic for 'wine',
yet Islam forbids even a taste
Unknown

•••

The good ship Temperance is headed for the port
Tony Benn

•••

Lips that touch liquor shall not touch ours
Kansas Ladies Prohibition Union

•••

To cease drinking is the easiest thing I ever did
I've done it a thousand times
Mark Twain

•••

Drunks who are terrified to read about the dangers of alcohol
should give up reading
Unknown

•••

When an alcoholic walks into a bar,
he may not have a drink, but it's still scary
Unknown

•••

Don't drink alone, people always find out
and it ruins your reputation
Rep Butler

•••

We are such things manure is made of,
so lets drink up and forget about it
Eugene O'Neill

•••

Friends & Enemies

I like dogs more than people
because dogs like you for yourself
John Paul Getty

•••

Dogs look up to men, cats look down on them
and pigs regard them as equal
Churchill

•••

Greater love hath no man than this,
that he should lay down his friend for his life
Bernard Levin

•••

Friends are worthless unless they can be used,
and when they are no longer useful they are not worth having
Armand Hammer

•••

Friendship bought with money does not last and yields nothing
Herman Melville

•••

The feigned friendship of the wolf is the most contemptible
Marcus Aurelius

•••

Sympathy is just a word in a dictionary,
you find it between shit and syphilis
Unknown

•••

A good listener is usually thinking about something else
Unknown

•••

If its possible its not a favour
Sam Goldwyn

•••

If you haven't any charity in your heart
you have the worst kind of heart trouble
Bob Hope

•••

Even people who didn't like Mohamed Ali liked him
Gus Damato

•••

Getting people to like you is only the reverse side of liking them
Norman Peale

•••

People only dislike in you what they hate in themselves
Lionel Blue

•••

Friends come and go but enemies accumulate
Thomas Jones Jnr

...

A man must be careful in his choice of enemies
Oscar Wilde

...

We were closer than friends,
we were enemies bound together in the same sin
Unknown

...

Its easier to forgive an enemy than a friend
Unknown

...

My father taught me to keep my friends close,
but to keep my enemies closer
Michael Corleone

...

When your enemy is up to his waist in water, pull him out
But if he is up to his chin drown him quickly
Baldesar Castegliogne

...

Never interfere with the enemy
when he is in the process of destroying himself
Napoleon Bonaparte

...

The best way to destroy your enemy
is to make him your friend
Abraham Lincoln

...

You can't shake hands with a clenched fist
Unknown

...

Everyone who shits on you is not necessarily your enemy,
and everyone who gets you out of the shit is not necessarily your friend
If you are warm and happy in a pile of shit,
keep your mouth shut
Unknown

...

Anger

The world would not exist without impudent people
so do not ask for impossibilities
Marcus Aurelius

...

A man must swallow a toad
to be sure of finding nothing more disgusting before the day is over
Chamforth

...

A drop of honey catches more flies than a gallon of gall
Abraham Lincoln

...

Anger is the mark of a weak mind
Diodetus

...

When a man fights it means a fool has lost his argument
Chinese

...

Never go to bed angry,
stay up and fight
Phyllis Diller

...

Time spent being angry is time lost
Unknown

...

Our anger is more detrimental than the things which anger us
Marcus Aurelius

...

If you keep your face to the sun
the shadows will always fall behind you
Unknown

...

When people say they are only being human
it usually means they are acting like beasts
Unknown

...

When men are inhuman to you,
take care not to feel the same towards them
Marcus Aurelius

•••

Don't be like a cushion
that bears the imprint of the last person who sits upon you
Unknown

•••

I've never hated a man enough to give him back his diamonds
Zsa Zsa Gabor

•••

A man who seeks revenge should dig two graves
Unknown

•••

Those who hate you only win if you hate them in return
And then you destroy yourself
Richard Nixon

•••

To refrain from imitation is the best revenge
Marcus Aurelius

•••

Ambition

I always wanted to be somebody
but I should have been more specific
Unknown

•••

Celebrities work hard all their lives to become well known,
And then wear dark glasses to avoid being recognized
Unknown

•••

Fame is so sweet
that men love anything connected with it, even death
Pascal

•••

An ambitious man will climb the crag
and walk in the mire
Sir Robert Chitta

•••

Be nice to people on your way up
because you'll meet them again on the way down
Wilson Mizner

•••

Nothing is impossible for the man who doesn't have to do it himself
Unknown

•••

Anyone who uses the phrase easy as taking candy from a baby,
has never tried taking candy from a baby
Unknown

•••

You can't build a reputation on what you are going to do
Unknown

•••

Yesterday's home runs don't win tomorrow's ball games
Frank Dick

•••

Aim for the stars;
you may never hit one but you will get used to aiming high
Armand Hammer

•••

If ambitious men find their way open they are busy not dangerous
But if their way is checked, they become secretly discontented
and look upon men with an evil eye
Francis Bacon

•••

It's amazing how much you can accomplish
if you do not care who gets the credit
Unknown

•••

It is more impressive
when others discover your good qualities without your help
Unknown

•••

He who wants everything will lose everything
Unknown

...

The man who covets is always poor
Claudian

...

Like a foolish man he flew to the bright light
and like a moth he burned his wings
Anthony Trollope

...

One must learn to itch in places one can scratch
Sancho Panza

...

The things we need in life are very few
Those we don't need are infinite,
and our desire for them is infinite too
Maimonides

...

I've never been in a room before with so many celebrities
I'm the only one here I've never heard of
Charity Hope Valentine

...

The morning a young man wakes and thinks he will never play the Dane,
his ambition ceases
Uncle Monty

...

From far below you will hear
the roar of a ruthless multitude of young men in a hurry;
in a hurry to get you out of the way
F M Cornforth

...

Success

Its nice to be important
but important to be nice
Rabbi Lionel Blue's auntie

...

Whatever you do,
the last impression is what people remember
Alma Fiersohn

•••

About eighty percent of success is just showing up
Woody Allen

•••

At an early age I learned two important facts,
first I had no talent and second this did not matter
Wilfred Hyde White

•••

Mediocrity has always found it easy to rise to the top in England
Thelma Holt

•••

Solitary trees grow not at all or to great heights
Winston Churchill

•••

If you are a self made man
it relieves the Almighty of a terrible responsibility
Theodore Roosevelt

•••

A successful man is a man who makes more money than his wife can spend
And a successful woman is a woman who can find such a man
Bienvenida Buck

•••

Its only eighteen inches between a pat on the back
and a kick in the pants
E Joseph Cossman

•••

There is nothing more destructive than success,
when it comes too early it ruins and when it comes too late it mocks
Gerontius

•••

Success and failure are both difficult to endure. Along with success
comes drugs, divorce, fornication, travel, medication, depression,
neurosis and suicide. With failure comes failure
Joseph Heller

•••

Success without honour is an unseasoned dish
It will satisfy your hunger but will not taste good
Joe Patern

•••

Glory is fleeting but obscurity lasts forever
Unknown

•••

Success is merely the postponement of failure
Graham Greene

•••

Success is an achievement
that covers up a multitude of blunders
George Bernard Shaw

•••

Practice even when success looks hopeless
Marcus Aurelius

•••

Sweat in training and box easy
Unknown

•••

Two wrongs are only the beginning
Unknown

•••

Even fingernails get in the way of a bad musician
Mexican

•••

God often presents fantastic opportunities
as brilliantly disguised problems
Unknown

•••

Obstacles are what you see
when you take your eye off the goal
Henry Ford

•••

You show me a good loser
and I'll show you a loser
Jimmy Carter

•••

My career started off badly, tapered off a bit in the middle
and the less said about the end the better
Edmund Blackadder

...

If you can't get to the top rung,
then stand on the bottom and shake the ladder
Libby Purves

...

Its a rat race
and the rats are winning
Tommy Docherty

...

Work

The closest you come to perfection
is in filling in a job application
Stanley Randall

...

A man who would be his own lawyer
has only a fool for a client
Lord Hailsham

...

It's a lawyers job to squeeze a man
And to squeeze him til he's squirming
Henry Hobson

...

A lawyer is someone
who helps you get what's coming to him
Unknown

...

Expecting every policeman to be honest
is like expecting every doctor to live forever
Unknown

...

However low a man sinks
He never reaches the level of the police
Quentin Crisp

•••

Being a convicted murderer
has the edge over being a solicitor
The Wimbledon Slaughterer

•••

A soldier's life is a life of honour
but a dog would not lead it
Prince Rupert of the Rhine

•••

An engineer is someone who can build for pound
what any fool can build for twenty
Unknown

•••

Actors are people who become bored
when the conversation is not about themselves
Unknown

•••

Acting is a profession
that thrives on malice
John Mortimer

•••

Actors eat too much and too fast,
for they know not when they eat again
Unknown

•••

A theatre director may think he's God,
but actors are all atheists
Unknown

•••

A great actor can bring tears to your eyes
but so can a car mechanic
Donald Reber

•••

No magician can produce a rabbit from the hat
if there is no rabbit in the hat
Boris Leomontov

•••

Anyone can be a fisherman in May
Santiago

...

All philosophers do
is contradict other philosophers
Unknown

...

Advertisers are the people
who rattle their sticks in the swill bucket
George Orwell

...

Gentlemen farmers are neither gentlemen nor farmers
Unknown

...

The difference between a good farmer and a bad farmer
might only be a week
Unknown

...

Medicine is a noble profession
but a damned bad business
Sir Humphrey Rolleston

...

The best surgeons are lazy and intelligent,
the worst are active and stupid. Between these are two other types,
but I've never worked out which is the better
Mervyn Rosenerg

...

There is a lot of difference between a good doctor and a bad one,
but little difference between a good one and none at all
Unknown

...

A consultant is a colleague called in at the last moment to share the blame
Unknown

...

A physician can bury his mistakes
but an architect can only advise his client to plant vines
Frank Lloyd Wright

...

If you have half a mind to go into teaching its probably all you need
Unknown

•••

Bankers are like everyone else, but richer
Unknown

•••

Accountants are witch doctors
and can to turn their hands to many kinds of magic
Lord Justice Harmer

•••

If vicars are too heavenly minded they are no earthly good
Unknown

•••

Dockers are charming fellows
but I cannot associate with them more than one at a time
Oscar Wilde

•••

We weren't the best band in the world
and when we played the national anthem,
people from many nations stood up
The Monkees

•••

Well spoken mature gentleman required until December 24th
Must have a happy disposition and be able to speak to children
Realistic costume provided.
Selfridges

•••

Hard work is the refuge of people
who have nothing whatever to do
Ocar Wilde

•••

He is so allergic to work
you must have seen him during a remission period
Sir John Stallworthy

•••

If things are hard to do they aren't worth doing
Homer Simpson

•••

If it works, fix it until it doesn't
Unknown

•••

Lazy people work twice as hard
John Paul Getty

•••

In the stationary business you have to get a move on
Coronation Street

•••

The person who comes to work with the flu
is the one who is after your job
Unknown

•••

I never did a day's work in my whole life;
it was all fun
Thomas A Edison

•••

For a living I race cars, play tennis and fondle women,
but I have weekends off and then I'm my own boss
Arthur

•••

Power

Nearly all men can stand adversity
but if you want to test a man's character give him power
Unknown

•••

It is a strange desire to seek power over others
and lose liberty over one's self. The rising into place is laborious
and by pains men come to greater pains
Francis Bacon

•••

For years I have patiently rolled this stone up hill,
but now it has rolled again to the bottom and I am 81 years old
Gladstone

•••

Its tough being a living legend
Ron Atkinson

...

Princes have much veneration but no rest
Francis Bacon

...

Losers stay put, but winners move up,
that is their fate
Unknown

...

The mill wheel turns for ever
and what is uppermost now remains not so
Berthold Brecht

...

The way up and the way down are the same
Heraclitus

...

Sit we upon the highest throne in the world
we sit only on our own tail
Montaigne

...

Having power is a bore
Not having it is a tragedy
Oscar Wilde

...

All power corrupts
but lack of power corrupts more
Unknown

...

Leadership

There can be no authority without mystery
since there is scant reverence for what is known well
Charles De Gaulle

...

No man is a hero to his valet
Thomas Stuttaford

...

People become immured to the debauches of their Emperor
so long as he builds roads and reduces taxes
Edward Gibbon

...

A leader is best when the people do not notice him
And when his task is done, they all say we did this
Chinese

...

The best leaders are made from clever idle men
Duke of Wellington

...

Never go into the office
until your staff have completed the Times crossword
Harold Macmillan

...

The world's problems would be solved instantly
if our leaders went to bed together naked
Allen Ginsburg

...

Two great princes who want to establish good relations
should never meet each other face to face
Philippe de Comines

...

The man of thought who will not act is ineffective,
the man of action who will not think is dangerous
Woodrow Wilson

...

I used to be indecisive but now I'm not so sure
Alan Partridge

...

The Duke of Somerset sympathised with the poor,
but this cost them more than other men's' indifference
G B Elton

...

If Number One trips he must be sustained,
if he makes mistakes they should be covered,
if he sleeps he must not be wantonly disturbed
and if he is no good he must be pole axed
Churchill

...

We walk through the corridors of power arm in arm,
but when we come to a door I go through first
Jim Hackett

...

Self delusion is essential in those who wish to lead
Guseppi di Lampeduso

...

An empty taxi drew up at the House of Commons
and who should get out but the leader of the Opposition
Winston Churchill

...

Good leaders do not simply react to public opinion
Otherwise we would still be hanging people in public
Lord Annen

...

Anyone can hold the helm when the sea is calm
Publius Syrus

...

Despots

Those intoxicated by power never willingly abandon it
Edmund Burke

...

There but for the grace of God goes God
Churchill

...

When the patient is ill the physician lets blood,
and when Russia is ill I am her physician
Ivan the Terrible

...

If anyone gives me a moments sorrow
I will give him a life time of misery
Yi Mo, Empress of China

•••

Si vous m'opposerai, je vous liquiderai
Churchill

•••

Adolph Hitler had the best answers to everything
Charles Manson

•••

Its a question of mind over matter,
I don't mind and you don't matter
Albany Police Chief

•••

The Shah of Iran allowed two political parties,
the Yes party and the Yes Sir party
Later these were combined into the Shah's party
Unknown

•••

If you give President Johnson your vote
he will always remember
But if you don't he'll never forget
Jack Valenti

•••

You are urging the wrong action my friend,
when you do not allow me to regard as the most learned of men,
the one with thirty legions
Fabrinus

•••

Appeasement to Hitler was like being nice to a crocodile
in the hope that he would eat you last
Churchill

•••

There are 3 kinds of despots, the despot who tyrannises the body,
the despot who tyrannises the soul and the despot who
tyrannises both. The first is called the Prince,
the second is the Pope and the third is the People
Oscar Wilde

•••

Tyranny is wanting to have by one means
what you can only have by another
Blaise Pascal

•••

A violent power
no man wields for long
Seneca

•••

His orders began to be carried out before they were given
or even before he had thought of them
And they always went much further than he would dare
Gabriel Garcia Marquez

•••

War & Peace

1969 was the only year in the last century
when a British soldier was not killed on active service
Unknown

•••

War is horrible but slavery is worse
and the British would rather die fighting than live in servitude
Churchill

•••

It never troubles the wolf how many sheep there be
Francis Bacon

•••

The brave will fight whatever the odds,
but cowards will always find a reason to lay down their weapons
Adolf Hitler

•••

Its not the size of the dog in the fight that matters
but the size of the fight in the dog
Cyril Smith

•••

It takes a brave man to be a coward
Harry Gregg
...

A man who most sincerely desires peace
will fight the hardest to achieve it
Alcebiades
...

Patriotism is the last refuge of the scoundrel
Unknown
...

The first casualty of war is truth
Hiram Johnson
...

There are three things you need to fight a war,
money, money, and money
Napoleon Bonaparte
...

The more you sweat in peace,
the less you bleed in war
Chinese
...

I don't know what weapons will be used in WW3,
but I can tell you that WW4 will be fought with stone clubs
Albert Einstein
...

To minimize the use of force and avoid barbarism,
British Army officers are selected from gentlemen
Patrick O'Connell
...

Remove the just grievances of the vanquished
before you disarm the victors
Churchill
...

A lost cause will always live in men's imagination,
and no British regiment has Culloden among its battle honours
John Prebble
...

In war the strong make slaves of the weak,
and in peace the rich make slaves of the poor
Unknown

•••

The strong do what they can
and the weak suffer what they must
Theucidydes

•••

Victory has a hundred fathers
but defeat is always an orphan
Unknown

•••

If our soldiers must fight they are too few,
and if they must die they are too many
Unknown

•••

I look upon the carcass of a man as I would look upon carcass of a horse
I do not know when this change happened, but I have changed
Union Soldier

•••

Peace is the period of cheating between conflicts
Unknown

•••

A prince should never make an aggressive alliance
with someone more powerful
If you are the victor you emerge as his prisoner
Machievelli

•••

I've buried the hatchets
but I can remember where I've buried them
Harold Wilson

•••

Once men reject a treaty
they cannot be expected to remember which clause they reject
A J P Taylor

•••

We shall sooner have the fowl
by hatching the egg than by smashing it
Abraham Lincoln

•••

The two greatest warriors are time and patience
Leo Tolstoy
•••

The only hope for perpetual peace is the grave
Immanuel Kant
•••

Politics

Politicians are like monkeys,
the higher they climb the more revolting parts they expose
Lloyd George
•••

Too bad ninety percent of politicians
give the other ten percent a bad name
Henry Kissenger
•••

The trouble with political jokes
is that half of them get elected
Unknown
•••

To describe the honourable member as a pest
would be unfair to pests
Nigel Lawson
•••

We have before us a rare sight indeed,
a rat reboarding the sinking ship
Gerald Kaufman
•••

Anyone can rat but it takes talent to re rat
Churchill
•••

If they last long enough, politicians, ugly buildings and whores
all end up respectable
Noah Cross
•••

If God had been a Liberal,
the ten commandments would have been the ten suggestions
Unknown

...

Finding constancy in Liberal policy
was like looking in a dark cupboard
for a black hole that wasn't there
Unknown

...

When the Democrats draw up a firing squad
they usually form up into a circle
Unknown

...

Think with the Liberals but eat with the Tories
Lord Henry Wotton

...

Tories dine on wine and grouse,
and Socialists on whining and grousing
Unknown

...

It cost the Congress party a fortune
to keep Gandhi in poverty
Unknown

...

Socialism is difficult to define
but you know it when you see it, like an elephant
Tony Benn

...

Socialists are the bland leading the bland
Unknown

...

Socialism would only work in Heaven where they don't need it,
or in Hell where they already have it
Unknown

...

In Germany you get yourself born
and the government does the rest
Jerome K Jerome

...

The National Socialists were against the Nationalists
and against the Socialists, and the People's Party
was against the people
Gunthar Grass

•••

Political influence is acquired in the same way as the gout
The method is to sit tight and drink port wine
F M Cornford

•••

If you can't ride two horses at the same time
you shouldn't be in the circus
Jimmy Knapp

•••

An English MP with a Scottish name representing
a Welsh constituency must be a canny fellow
Edward Heath

•••

Tactics are knowing what to do when there is something to do
Strategy is knowing what to do when there is nothing to do
Sir Trevor Holsworth

•••

When you come to a fork in the road, take it
Yogi Bear

•••

If you keep your head when those around you are losing theirs,
maybe you don't know what's going on
John Cole

•••

Our Chancellor has a fatal flaw,
he's always wrong
Ian McCleod

•••

Nothing is hated more in politics
than being right too soon
Brian Waldren

•••

If nothing else works,
a stubborn pigheaded refusal to face the facts usually helps
Edmund Blackadder

•••

My political problems were insoluble
and my economic ones were incomprehensible
Alec Douglas Home

...

Being a minister is like being a mushroom;
they keep you in the dark and periodically throw manure over you
Unknown

...

The West Lothian Question
is like squaring the circle or hunting the snark,
it's a riddle wrapped in a mystery inside an enigma
Simon Jenkins

...

We tend to meet any new situation by reorganising
and how wonderfully this can create the illusion of progress
Petronius

...

Violence should be inflicted once and for all,
people then forget what it tastes like and are less resentful
Benefits should be conferred gradually
as in that way they taste better
Machievelli

...

When you have a man by the balls
his heart and mind are sure to follow soon
Richard Nixon

...

The prince should delegate to others
the enactment of unpopular measures
and keep in his own hands the distribution of favours
Machievelli

...

There are two institutions you must never oppose;
the Roman Catholic Church and the National Union of Mineworkers
Stanley Baldwin

...

Never wrestle with a pig,
the pig likes it and you both get dirty
Unknown

...

Its only in politics where you can have your cake and eat it
and still lose weight
Unknown

•••

Politicians who stand in the middle of the road get run over
Aneurin Bevan

•••

Either compromise and influence people
or stay pure and stand alone
Jeremy Vine

•••

Eventually those who compromise are compromised out of existence
John Prescott

•••

There are two kinds of political forecasters, those who don't know,
and those who don't know they don't know
J K Galbraith

•••

The iron law of politics is the survival of the slickest
Andrew Martin

•••

In politics, whilst there is death there is hope
John Paul Getty

•••

Civil Service

Successful diplomacy is the ability to tell a man to go to hell
and for him to look forward to the journey
Unknown

•••

A compromise is where you divide the cake
so everyone believes they have the biggest piece
Unknown

•••

An ambassador is an honest man
who is sent abroad to lie for his country
Sir Henry Wotton

•••

When a diplomat says yes, he means perhaps,
and when he says perhaps he means no
If he says no he's no diplomat
If a lady says no, she means maybe
and if she says maybe, she means yes
If she says yes she's no lady
Unknown

•••

It may not be diplomatic to tell the whole truth but never tell a lie
This will always be found out and will undermine confidence
Sir John Thompson

•••

The soul of diplomacy is dining
Lord Palmerston

•••

The function of civil servants
is to listen to their ministers dropping bricks
Clement Atlee

•••

If the outcome is good the minister takes the credit
and if it is bad the civil servant takes the blame
Metropolitan Commissioner of Police

•••

Washington is where three hundred thousand people
come to work each day, and after coffee
write a memo to someone who sent them a memo yesterday
Unknown

•••

How many people work in there,
asked a tourist outside the Ministry of Health building
About half replied the policeman on duty
Austen Bradford Hill

•••

Democracy

The people's judgment is not always true,
the most can err as grossly as the few
John Dryden

•••

Democracy is where the votes of two idiots
count more than the vote of one wise man
Adolph Hitler

•••

Democracy takes time;
dictatorship is quicker but more people get shot
Harry Perkins

•••

No democracy survives long
that does not recognise the rights of minorities
Franklin D Roosevelt

•••

In a democracy, men do not seek authority so they may impose a policy
they seek a policy so they may achieve authority
Unknown

•••

She turned to politics to express her inclination
to make people do what was good for them
Unknown

•••

Committees are contrivances by which persons
who separately can take no effective action
decide that no effective action should be taken
Unknown

•••

A committee is a group of the unwilling
chosen from the unfit to do the unnecessary
Unknown

•••

The less you enjoy committees, the more you are pressed to join them
Unknown

•••

The length of a committee meeting
increases with the square of the number of members present
Shanahan's Law

•••

The time a committee spends on an item
is inversely proportional to its cost
Unknown

•••

The best committee has two members with one away ill
Unknown

•••

A committee is a meeting where the minutes are kept
and the hours are lost
Unknown

•••

Public Opinion

One fifth of the people are against everything all of the time
R F Kennedy

•••

Elections are won
because most people vote against someone, not for them
Franklin Adams

•••

People long for two things;
for bread and circuses
Diogenes Laertus

•••

The public buys its opinions as it buys meat and milk;
on the basis that its cheaper than keeping a cow
Samuel Butler

•••

It's a pity all the people who know how to run the country
are too busy driving taxi cabs or cutting hair
George Burns

•••

Britain has produced thousands of blameless greengrocers
but not one blameless monarch
George Bernard Shaw

•••

I did not come to Washington to be liked
and I was not disappointed
Senator Phil Gamm

•••

The people of France might be impressed by a politician
if he were crucified and rose again on the third day
Talleyrand

•••

Never confuse political influence with public esteem
Kenneth Baker

•••

Liberty

When people are free to do as they please
they usually imitate each other
Unknown

•••

A free society is where its is safe to be unpopular
Unknown

•••

Liberty equality and fraternity are the grandest nonsense,
liberty automatically precludes equality
Adolph Hitler

•••

Liberty should be rationed
for those with the talent to enjoy it
Noel Marquis de Maine

•••

Those who want the freedom of the jungle
should accept its retribution without yelping
Edward de Bono

•••

The dangers of freedom are appalling
Lytton Strachey

•••

If slaves are to wait for liberty until they become wise,
they may have to wait forever
Macaulay

•••

Slavery is like holding a wolf by the ears,
you may not like it but you dare not let it go
Thomas Jefferson

•••

Tolerance is the result of boredom, not enlightenment
Quentin Crisp

•••

Public Speaking

The right to be heard
does not include the right to be taken seriously
Unknown

•••

A politician must often talk
before he has thought and read
Thomas Macaulay

•••

It takes me about three weeks to prepare a good impromptu speech
Mark Twain

•••

He sent words into the darkness like soldiers into battle
and was never short of reinforcements
John Mortimer

•••

When ideas fail, words come in very handy
Unknown

•••

A little inaccuracy can save a ton of explanation
Unknown

•••

Beware the man whose native tongue is ambiguity
Unknown

•••

The only reason it takes him so long is that having nothing to say
he finds it difficult to know when he is finished
John Major

•••

There are two kinds of people,
those who finish what they start, and so on
Unknown

•••

Of those who say nothing, few are silent
Unknown

•••

No one has a finer command of the language
than the person who keeps his mouth shut
Sam Rayburn

•••

It is better to remain silent and appear a fool
than to speak out and remove all doubts
Unknown

•••

Whales are not harpooned until they spout
Dennis Thatcher

•••

He had a majestic turn of phrase
and often spoke for long periods without saying anything
Thomas Macaulay

•••

He is the talking equivalent of invisible ink
and within seconds of him speaking
you cannot recall a word he has said
Matthew Parris

•••

The first half of what he said meant something different
and the second half meant nothing at all
Tom Stoppard

•••

When in doubt mumble, when in trouble delegate,
and when in charge ponder
Borens Law

•••

A Foreign Secretary's speech is either dull or dangerous
Harold Macmillan

•••

The best speech sounds better every time you hear it
Unknown

•••

A good speech should be like a bikini;
it should be brief but cover all the important parts,
yet leave something still to contemplate
Unknown

•••

It really is annoying that you should steal my jokes,
but for you to proceed to ruin them is doubly so
Unknown

•••

One stands a higher chance of being foolish
when one is guided by high principles
Lord Melbourne

•••

Think twice before you speak
and you'll find everyone talking about something else
F Kitman

•••

When the going gets tough the tough get profane
Unknown

...

Writing

If I have to go down, I'll go down writing
Unknown

...

Every man should have a son, plant a tree and write a book
Confuscius

...

Christ was a great teacher but he published nothing
Unknown

...

Originality is only undetected plagiarism
W R Inge

...

Your manuscript is both good and original;
but the part that is good is not original
and the part that is original is not good
Samuel Johnson

...

When a thing has been said well,
have no scruples and copy it
Anatole France

...

When people ask for criticism
what they really want is praise
W S Maugham

...

All an author wants is 6000 words of closely reasoned adulation
Tony Jay

...

They say that critics can be bought,
and as far as I can see they are not expensive
Unknown

•••

Short words are the best and old words are the best of all
Churchill

•••

People are fed up with the same old clichés,
what they need is some new ones
Sam Goldwyn

•••

English is a strange language
in which a fat chance and a slim chance are the same thing
J G White

•••

We have lost the facility of giving lovely names to things,
and the man who calls a spade a spade should be compelled to use one
Oscar Wilde

•••

A synonym is a word you use
when you can't spell the word you first thought of
Unknown

•••

Prose is words in the best order,
poetry is the best words in the best order
Coleridge

•••

To write poetry, just choose a good prose source
and do to it what Shakespeare did to Sir Thomas North
David West

•••

There's nothing to writing,
all you do is sit down at a typewriter and open a vein
Red Smith

•••

What can be said at all can be said clearly
Ludwig Wittgenstein

•••

If you want to mean what you say
you must learn to say what you mean
Reginald Johnson

•••

To communicate effectively,
first simplify and then exaggerate
Unknown

•••

Good writers write novels, adequate ones write biographies
and bad ones write newspapers
Roy Hudd

•••

The purpose of journalism is to comfort the afflicted
and afflict the comfortable
Unknown

•••

Journalists always write with other men's blood
Unknown

•••

Newspaper editors separate the wheat from the chaff
and then publish the chaff
Adlai Stevenson

•••

Journalism is what wraps the cinders the following day
Unknown

•••

A good novel tells you the truth about its hero,
a bad novel tells you the truth about its author
Unknown

•••

Whilst writing a book, the best way to earn a living,
is as a railway crossing keeper where there is only one train a day
John Betjeman

•••

No one but a fool would write for anything except money
John Charrington

•••

Keep a diary and one day it may keep you
Mae West

•••

You should not expect payment
for writing a love letter
Unknown

•••

A good story should start with an earthquake
and work up to a climax
Sam Goldwyn

•••

The best books are those that tell you what you already know
George Orwell

•••

What is written without effort is read without pleasure
Dr Johnson

•••

If your writing doesn't keep you up at night
it won't keep anyone else up either
James Keynes

•••

True ease in writing comes from art not chance,
as those who move easiest have learned to dance
Alexander Pope

•••

This letter is longer than usual,
I did not have time to write a shorter one
Blaise Pascal

•••

Never do anything irreversible; don't get a criminal record,
don't have an unwanted child, and don't write a book you regret
Unknown

•••

The difference between a joist and a girder,
is that joist wrote Ulysses and girder wrote Faust
Irish

•••

The writer does his work alone and if he is good enough
he must face eternity or the lack of it each day
Ernest Hemingway

•••

Good writers are people who find writing difficult
Unknown

•••

The establishment's attitude to the Great War made me realise
that I had always been just what a writer should be - an outsider
A Conan Doyle

•••

If I knew why I write I wouldn't need to write
Paul Austen

•••

Writing is an attempt to reach others and make them love you

Anita Brookner

•••

Now that I know the meaning of life
I have no more need to write
Oscar Wilde

•••

Love

Putting first things first
Thousands have lived without love
Not one without water
W H Auden

•••

Love is fire and flame for a year, then ashes for thirty
Unknown

•••

Love is so subtly insane
that only humans are clever enough to fall into it
Dudley Young

•••

It is impossible to love and to be wise
Francis Bacon

...

Love is the delusion
that all men and women are different
Unknown

...

Beauty is the wonder of wonders
and only shallow people do not judge by appearances
Oscar Wilde

...

A man is charmed through his eyes, a woman by what she hears
So no man need be anxious about his age
Laurie Lee

...

When a woman is speaking to you
listen to what she says with her eyes
Victor Hugo

...

A loving wife is better than making fifty at cricket or even ninety nine
But beyond that I will not go
Unknown

...

I feel sorry for those who never get their hearts desire
but sorrier still for those who do
Oscar wilde

...

A man can be happy with any woman,
as long a he does not love her
Oscar Wilde

...

It is a mistake to confuse happiness with one person
Anita Brookner

...

Why love when losing hurts so much
C S Lewis

...

Two people in love are unknowing actors set to play
Romeo and Juliet by a director who conceals that
the tomb and the poison are already in the script
Guseppi di Lampeduso

...

Most marital arguments are about money,
so agree the price at the start
Unknown

...

Love is nice but its nicer with noodles
Lionel Blue

...

For the middle classes, love is a hobby
Christopher Isherwood

...

The biggest difference between people
is not whether they are rich or poor,
but whether they have known love,
or whether they have not
Tennessee Williams

...

Love has driven men and women to curious extremes
It led Juliet to feign death and Ophelia to madness
No doubt it disturbed the serenity of the Garden of Eden
And we are told it started the Trojan War
John Mortimer

...

I fall in love constantly and indiscriminately,
the effect is the same as if I never fall in love at all
André Moreau

...

Love is nothing without liberty
Rigoletto

...

If you want something, set it free
and if it returns its yours forever
If it doesn't it was never yours
Unknown

...

Children begin by loving their parents
As they grow older they judge them;
sometimes they forgive them
Oscar Wilde

...

The minute you have children
you forgive your parents everything
Susan Hill

...

To love oneself is the beginning of a lifelong romance
Oscar Wilde

...

The more I love mankind the less I love man
Shopenhauer

...

Women & Men

Women are people with sexual organs over their hearts
Leo Tolstoy

...

The useless piece of flesh at the end of the penis
is a man
Unknown

...

The only thing to do with women
is to make love to them if they are pretty,
and to someone else if they are not
Oscar Wilde

...

If you have a grandmother with one eye in the middle of her head,
you don't keep her in the living room
Lyndon Johnson

...

The best ten years of a woman's life
are between the ages of twenty nine and thirty
Peter Weiss

•••

Whoever called women the fair sex
knew nothing about justice
Unknown

•••

To wear too much rouge and not quite enough clothes
is always a sign of despair in a woman
Lord Arthur Goring

•••

It is better to be beautiful than to be good,
but better to be good than to be ugly
Unknown

•••

Dress well and they notice the dress,
dress impeccably and they notice the woman
Coco Chanel

•••

Fashion is a form of ugliness so intolerable
that we have to alter it every 6 months
Unknown

•••

If Cleopatra's nose had been shorter,
the whole of history would have been different
Blaise Pascal

•••

Women would be more charming
if you could fall into their arms
without falling into their hands
Ambrose Pierce

•••

It is hell with women and worse without them
Unknown

•••

Most girls of 19 are randy little minxes
who give small thought that the man might be married to someone else
Alan Clarke

•••

Only good girls keep diaries;
bad ones don't have the time
Tallulah Bankhead

•••

A girl must be like a blossom, with honey for just one man
A man must be like the honey bee, and gather all he can
To fly from blossom to blossom, a honeybee must be free
but blossom must never ever fly from bee to bee to bee
The King of Siam

•••

A man may seek the purity of the Lily
but he would be inhuman
if he refused the other flowers along the roadside
Barbara Cartland

•••

A very little wit is valued in a woman,
as we are pleased with a few words spoken plainly by a parrot
Jonathon Swift

•••

Women represent the triumph of matter over mind,
just as men represent the triumph of mind over morals
Oscar Wilde

•••

When a woman inclines to learning
there is usually something wrong with her sexual apparatus
Frederich Nietzsche

•••

German ladies are brilliantly educated, and by the age of eighteen
have forgotten more than the average English woman has ever read
Jerome K Jerome

•••

Older women hold themselves together with hairpins and corsets
and disguise themselves with lipstick and mascara
Unknown

•••

Women are not allowed to belch or fart or snore,
and if they didn't bitch a little they'd explode
Unknown

•••

Men who hang around ladies' lavatories
are asking to have their illusions shattered
Peter Greenaway

...

In the German language
a young lady has no sex, but a turnip has
Mark Twain

...

The greater the man
the more insignificant should be his woman
Adolph Hitler

...

There are only two places for women,
on a pedestal or as a doormat
Pablo Picasso

...

Women are like modern paintings
You'll never enjoy them if you try to understand them
Freddie Bulsara

...

Daughter she obey her father, wife she obey her husband,
and widow she obey her son
Vietnamese

...

For centuries Burmese women have always walked behind the men
But this changed after the war, when the country
became littered with land mines
Unknown

...

Whatever women do,
they must do twice as well as men, to be thought half as good
Fortunately this is not difficult
Charlotte Whittons

...

Only women and horses work for nothing
Doug Ellis

...

Women constitute 1/2 the world's population, perform 2/3 of the work,
receive 1/10 of the income and own 1/100 of the property
United Nations

...

A dirty man smells like a dog and a dirty woman smells like a cat
But who is it that washes the clothes and cleans the bath
Unknown

...

A man should never have a garden
that is too big for his wife to keep up
Unknown

...

Just about the time a woman thinks her work is done,
she becomes a grandmother
Unknown

...

Women can do anything and ladies can do it in style
Californian

...

The old man thought of the sea as a woman,
as someone who gave or withheld great favours
Both are affected by the moon
Ernest Hemingway

...

In the hive and the anthill
we see the two things some of us most dread,
the dominance of the female and the collective
C S Lewis

...

Certain women should be struck regularly like gongs
Noel Coward

...

A woman, a dog and a walnut tree,
the more you beat them the better they be
American

...

There are only two things wrong with men,
everything they do and everything they say
Unknown

...

Male car drivers should not be allowed,
even God says She regrets them
Unknown

...

Women should judge men and forgive them
Unknown

...

In trying to make themselves angels men become beasts
Michel de Montaigne

...

Old men like to give advice to console them
for no longer being able to set a bad example
La Rouchefoucauld

...

If God had meant the sexes to get on well together,
why did he make men impossible
Unknown

...

Marriage

Avoid love at all costs,
it will only lead you to the tomb of marriage
Giacomo Puccinni

...

To St Paul, marriage was barely preferable to Hell
To women these two states may be the same
But either is more preferable than work
Quentin Crisp

...

Marriage isn't a word it's a sentence
Unknown

...

Courtship is the period during which
the girl decides if she can do better
Unknown

•••

My wives married me;
I didn't marry them
J Paul Getty

•••

When a girl marries she exchanges the attention of many men
for the inattention of one
Helen Rowland

•••

Why does my wife want a new dress,
I never take her out
Groucho Marx

•••

A little incompatibility is the spice of life
as long as one partner has income and the other has pattability
Ogden Nash

•••

These are the horrors of home life; the dusting, sweeping, harrowing,
scrubbing, waxing, waning, washing, mangolling, drying, mowing, clipping,
raking, rolling, shovelling, grinding, pounding, banging, and slamming
Samuel Beckett

•••

Never marry a man hoping you will change him
It never happens
Unknown

•••

Carnal marriages begin in happiness and end in strife
Lord Cecil

•••

Men are rapists and women are whores
Marriage simply legitimises the arrangement
Unknown

•••

When a man marries his mistress
he creates a vacancy
James Goldsmith

•••

If you have a perfect marriage
find another one quickly
Unknown

•••

Southern American marriages are always happy;
its the living together afterwards that the trouble
Unknown

•••

Three kinds of husbands are deceived by their wives,
the first is born to it, the second doesn't know
and the third doesn't care
Unknown

•••

When a woman remarries it is because she detested her first husband
When a man remarries it means he adored his first wife
Women try their luck, men risk theirs
Oscar Wilde

•••

More marriages would survive
if partners realised the better comes after the worse
Doug Larson

•••

The difference between a successful marriage and an unsuccessful one,
could be leaving just three or four things a day unsaid
Harlen Miller

•••

Twenty years of romance leaves a woman looking like a ruin
Twenty years of marriage leaves her looking like a public building
Unknown

•••

The Gay community will be piling into marriage
just when the rest of us are giving it up
Gore Vidal

•••

In Saudi Arabia women who commit adultery get stoned
In America women who get stoned commit adultery
Unknown

•••

It is better to marry a young girl and satisfy her curiosity,
than to marry a widow and disappoint her
Groucho Marx

...

Divorce is like Armageddon;
there are no winners just a lot of ruins
Unknown

...

Sex

To Vauxhall Gardens they do come,
some to undo and some to be undone
Henry Fielding

...

There are two places where love making is not ridiculous,
on stage where it is meant to be seen but not felt,
and in marriage where it is meant to be felt but not seen
Nirad Chaudhuri

...

Always try to go to bed with a good Trollope
Harold Macmillan

...

The perfect woman would make love until four in the morning,
and then turn into a pizza
Unknown

...

Women need a good reason to have sex;
men just need a good place
Unknown

...

O innocent victim of cupid, remember this terse little verse
To let a fool kiss you is stupid; to let a kiss fool you is worse
E Y Harburg

...

Kissing is only out of season
when the gorse is out of flower
Unknown

...

I used to be Snow White but I drifted
Mae West

...

I knew Doris Day before she was a virgin
Theatre critic

...

Never in the history of sex
was so much offered to so many by so few
Quentin Crisp

...

When a young soldier ravished a sacred Indian cow,
the case was dismissed when the cow was cited in a previous case
Spike Millegan

...

Men who cannot close their eyes when they make love
are condemned to pursue beautiful women
Unknown

...

Incest is all right
as long as you keep it in the family
Olivier Todd

...

Don't knock masturbation;
its sex with the person you like best
Unknown

...

If you feel sexy,
do unto yourself what you would do unto others
Unknown

...

It is folly to give girls of sixteen contraceptives,
and folly not to
David Mercer

...

Contraceptives should be used on every conceivable occasion
Spike Millegan

•••

Men don't like taking a shower
with men who like taking a shower with men
Unknown

•••

British society is governed by three things, thuggery, muggery
and I've written a book about the third
A L Rowse

•••

Try everything there is to try
Just in case you're missing something
Russ Conway

•••

Homosexuality is as English as Morris dancing
but infinitely less tedious
Oscar Wilde

•••

I prefer not to thrust my sexuality
down other people's throats
Unknown

•••

He spent one night under Venus
and the rest of his life under Mercury
Gustaf Flaubert

•••

Life is a sexually transmitted disease
Toilet graffiti

•••

On his wedding night a woman's fifth husband may know what to do,
but not how to make it interesting
Unknown

•••

If you have lots of money always get a hooker
You owe them nothing and they can't ring you back
Frank Sinatra

•••

Nations

There is no more wretched occupation
than trying to make the English laugh
Malcolm Muggeridge

...

The English would rather have Typhoid
than have a good time
Oscar Wilde

...

The British are a law abiding nation
and if asked to storm a railway station
would first buy a platform ticket
Lenin

...

The English always play the game
but change the rules if they're losing
Harold Lasky

...

The sun never set on the British Empire
because God didn't trust the British in the dark
Unknown

...

The English make excellent butlers but poor waiters
Unknown

...

Englishmen only acknowledge strangers
if there no chance of a conversation with them
That is why they wave at trains
Unknown

...

If you want to get on well with the British
you must first have a devil of a row with them
Joshua Slocum

...

The Pilgrim Farters created a stink in Britain
and ran away to America
Seven year old

...

Britain is a land of mists and powerful middle classes
Benjamin Disraeli

•••

Britain is the largest island known to Rome
Its sky is overcast with continuous rain and cloud
Tacitus

•••

England is made of coal and surrounded by fish
and it would take a genius to engineer a shortage of either
Aneurin Bevan

•••

If the English can dismiss a minister for an affair with a slip of a girl
they are clearly not ready to join the Common Market
La Monde

•••

An Englishman's mind works best when its almost too late
Helmut Schmidt

•••

The day the world ends I would like to be in England
because there everything happens ten years too late
Heinrich Heinman

•••

A man who speaks many languages is called multilingual;
a man who speaks one language is called English
Unknown

•••

The British invented cricket
to give atheists some idea of eternity
Unknown

•••

A Cardigan man can buy in Jerusalem and sell in Aberdeen
and still make a profit
Unknown

•••

Kentish born and Kentish bred, strong in the arm
and weak in the head
Unknown

•••

Swansea was a group of small villages held together by gossip
Dylan Thomas

•••

An acre in Middlesex is better than a principality in Utopia
Thomas Macaulay

•••

The Studland peninsula is where you can find all 6 British reptiles;
the grass snake, smooth snake, adder, slow worm,
common lizard and Michael Portillo
Bill Bryson

•••

Birmingham is the city
where the concrete never sets
Unknown

•••

In Scotland they have three seasons,
April, May and Winter
Unknown

•••

When a man in a dress starts to strangle a cat,
it means that Scottish dinner is served
Unknown

•••

The Scots have short arms and deep pockets
Robert McNeil

•••

The finest prospect a Scotsman ever sees
is the high road to England
Dr Johnson

•••

A Scottish croft is a small piece of land
surrounded by regulations
Unknown

•••

All the best fools come from Ireland
but only a greater one would want to go there
Elizabeth I

•••

Ireland is the old sow that eats her farrow
Stephen Daedalus

•••

Put an Irishman on the spit
and you can always find another Irishman to turn it
G B Shaw

•••

At the bottom of every Irish heart is a little bag of bile
Harold Nicholson

•••

If you don't like the island,
a boat leaves in the morning
Signeur of Sark

•••

America is made with cardboard and lit with neon lights
Malcolm Muggeridge

•••

Britannia rules the waves
and America waives the rules
Unknown

•••

Americans wish you to succeed, and hope you will drag them forward too
The British wish you to fail for fear you may leave them behind
Quentin Crisp

•••

The Statue of Liberty was made by a Dago on behalf of the French,
to welcome the Irish to the Dutch city of New York
O'Henry

•••

There are 60 million Americans who can't read
and equal number who don't bother
Unknown

•••

New Mexico deported a monkey to Texas
and this increased the average IQ of both states
Unknown

•••

Texas is where folk know when you're sick and care when you die
Lyndon Johnson

•••

Dallas was all Macdonalds, American football
and teenage going steady bracelets
Lynn Harrel

•••

The place is always packed these days
No wonder no one wants to go there any more
Sam Goldwyn

•••

If America ever needed an enema
they'd stick the hose up Louisiana
Unknown

•••

In Oregon, when you see Mount Ranier it is going to rain,
and when you can't see Mount Ranier its already raining
Unknown

•••

America must be tilted
because everything loose ends up in California
Unknown

•••

La Jolla is where old people take their parents to live
Raymond Chandler

•••

I don't know where Canada is,
or even which street its in
Al Capone

•••

The Germans are hungry
even when they are full
Gunthar Grass

•••

The Hun is always at your throat or at your feet
Churchill

•••

In Germany it is a proud father
that has a scarred son
Fred Zimmerman

...

In 1930, German fairy godmothers
could bestow intelligence, honesty or fascism,
but only two out of three
Unknown

...

The Swiss have no enemies
but they also have no friends
Unknown

...

Italian is the language of song
And Irish is the voice of flattery
Quentin Crisp

...

In Italy they take care of the small things
and the big things take care of themselves
Unknown

...

Rome reminds me of the man
who made a living exhibiting his grandmother's corpse
James Joyce

...

Italian Alzheimers Disease is when you forget everything
except a grudge
Unknown

...

The vanity of Sicilians is stronger than their misery
They consider themselves perfect and have no wish to improve
Guseppi di Lampedusa

...

The worst European would have German humour,
Spanish humility, French honesty, English cookery,
Irish sobriety and Scottish generosity
Unknown

...

The French will eat anything that slithers, crawls or hops
Unknown

•••

There is an opinion that the French are wiser than they seem
and the Spanish seem wiser than they are
Francis Bacon

•••

Antisemitism is endemic in Austria,
it simply surfaces each time they have a crisis
Fred Zimmerman

•••

Antisemitism is eternal, like gravity
One can assume there is antisemitism on Mars
Paul Bodor

•••

There a three things God should not have created,
Persians, Jews and flies
Saddam Hussein

•••

Hungarians and Romanians would both offer to sell you their sister,
but only the Hungarian would deliver
Unknown

•••

Albania was a sort of holiday camp without any facilities
Louise de Berniers

•••

In the Afghan dictionary,
"gratitude" is found after "gimme and gotcher"
Frank Anderson

•••

Vietnam is a snake; treat it kindly and it will refresh you,
but tread on it and you had better watch out
Keith Floyd

•••

Russia is never so strong or as weak as foreigners might think
Unknown

•••

The Soviets will feel less encircled
when they have conquered more than half the world
Unknown

...

The Chinese have forgotten more
than the rest of us have ever known
Unknown

...

The Chinese will eat anything
that has four legs and is not a table
Unknown

...

What the horns are to the buffalo,
the paw is to the tiger and the sting is to the bee,
so deceit is to the Bengali
Macaulay

...

The sign outside the factory in Ghaziobad read,
"H Hussain and Sons, Forgers and Fabricators"
Unknown

...

When I see what is on offer in Indian bookstalls,
I am grateful that so many of my fellow countrymen are illiterate
Gandhi

...

Laos was an expensive American joke,
a motiveless place where nothing is made and everything is imported
Paul Theroux

...

In Manilla it takes the police no time at all
to reach the scene of a crime
They are often already there when its committed
Unknown

...

The Australian accent is like Cockney
with your mouth shut to stop the flies getting in
Unknown

...

So fell Peru. We gave them hunger, greed and the cross;
the three great gifts of civilisation
Peter Schafer

•••

Poor Mexico, so far from heaven
and so close to the USA
Unknown

•••

An honest Mexican is one who stays bought
John Gunther

•••

There is no greater sorrow than to be blind in Granada
Unknown

•••

Suburbia is where the developers bulldoze the trees
and name the streets after themselves
Unknown

•••

In the country people get up early because they have so much to do,
and go to bed early because there is so little to talk about
Oscar Wilde

•••

Social classes

Good breeding consists of concealing how much we think of ourselves
and how little we think of other people
Unknown

•••

Its nice to be in the same boat as one's betters,
especially if its sinking
Quentin Crisp

•••

The power and privileges of the upper classes
are not inherited through superior genes
Hubert Bowles

•••

When I want a peerage
I will pay for it like an honest man
Alfred Harnsworth

•••

I am not going to pay good money
to join a club that lets in people like me
Groucho Marx

•••

It is one thing to condemn privilege
but quite another to refuse it
Lenin

•••

Only domestic servants apologise
Alan Clark

•••

You can't make the poor richer by making the rich poorer
Nigel Lawson

•••

The only way to get the rich to work harder is to pay them more,
and the only way to get the poor to work harder is to pay them less
Rodney Bickerstaff

•••

What we want
is more schoolmasters, wool weavers, tailors and builders
What we have instead
is more footmen, gamekeepers, jockeys and prostitutes
G B Shaw

•••

The middle classes are those who can maintain their standard of living
for 3 years after losing their job
Unknown

•••

The implicit ambition of the middle classes is to avoid manual labour
Arthur Miller

•••

My parents were of the lower upper middle class
This is essentially the middle class that has no money
George Orwell

•••

We were poor but we had a piano,
so I suppose we were middle class
Unknown

•••

I'd like to live like a poor man,
but with lots of money
Pablo Picasso

•••

Give courage to a peasant
and he will soon jump into bed with you
Unknown

•••

The only classless thing about horse racing
is that it attracts the worst elements of all classes
Unknown

•••

No one can make you feel inferior without your consent
Eleanor Roosevelt

•••

Time

When God made time he made plenty of it
Robin Neillands

•••

Voyageur II left the solar system in 1989 travelling at 33,000 mph
Its next encounter is with a small red star called Ross 248,
in the year 42,165 AD
Unknown

•••

The Swiss manufacture time, the French hoard it, Italians want it,
Americans say its money and Hindus say it doesn't exist
Peter Lorraine

•••

You can't measure time the way you measure money,
dollars are all the same but each day is different
Jorge Louis Borges
•••

Time is too slow for those who wait, too swift for those who fear,
too long for those who grieve, too short for those rejoicing
But for those who love, time is eternity
Henry van Dyke
•••

When I was a child I laughed and wept, time crept
When as a youth I dreamed and talked, time walked
When I became a full grown man, time ran
And later as I older grew time flew
Soon I shall find while travelling on, time gone
Will Christ have saved my soul by then,   Amen
Chesterfield Cathedral Clock
•••

Time is the sentimentalist of the four dimensions
Constance Lambert
•••

A man with a watch knows what time it is
but a man with two watches is never sure
Unknown
•••

Even a stopped clock tells the right time twice every day
Withnail
•••

An alarm clock is a device
for waking people who do not have small children
Unknown
•••

Time flies like an arrow
and fruit flies like a banana
Unknown
•••

Some people can stay longer in an hour
than others can in a week
William Deane Howells
•••

I've finished my course of speed reading
and I read War and Peace in fifteen minutes
Its all about Russia
Woody Allen

•••

A tortoise was mugged by a snail
but couldn't remember the details because it was over too quickly
Unknown

•••

If time travel could exist, it already would
Unknown

•••

The distinction between past and present and future
is only an illusion
Albert Einstein

•••

You cannot step twice in the same river
Heraclitus

•••

Everything oozes, its never the same pus
from one day to the next
Samuel Beckett

•••

Mondays are a terrible way to spend one seventh of one's life
Unknown

•••

History is just one damned thing after another
Henry Ford

•••

Manners require time
and nothing is more vulgar than haste
Ralph Waldo Emerson

•••

Beware the lust to finish something
Unknown

•••

The surest way to be late is to have plenty of time
Leo Kennedy

•••

The less one has to do, the less time one has to do it
Earl of Chesterfield

•••

This work not done and these five minutes gone my friend
We shall not have these five minutes again
Gordon of Khartoum

•••

He's a perfectly intolerable man who doesn't know the difference
between 6 o'clock and 1 minute past 6
W H Auden

•••

Men count up the faults
of those who keep them waiting
Unknown

•••

The past should be a springboard, not a hammock
Irene Ball

•••

Wedged as we are between two eternities of idleness,
there is no excuse to be idle now
Anthony Burgess

•••

Time is the great teacher that kills all its pupils
Hector Berlioz

•••

What comes to an end is always brief
Unknown

•••

Time goes by you say but no
Alas its time that stays, and us who go
Austin Dobson

•••

Oh for and engine to keep back all the clocks
Ben Johnson

•••

Six hours sleep is enough for a man,
seven for a woman and eight for a fool
King George III

•••

Whoever thinks of going to bed before midnight is a scoundrel
Samuel Johnson

...

I enjoy getting up in the morning so much
I often go back to bed just for the chance to do it again
Claude Monet

...

Things are not what they used to be,
and what is more, they never were what they used to be
Robert Graves

...

If things are to stay as they are, then they must change
Guseppi di Lampedusa

...

Look upon change as something you can rely on
and it will become a comfort
Unknown

...

Life itself can't give you joy unless you really will it
Life just gives you time and space
Its up to you to fill it
The Voice of AFN

...

Life is a wonderful precious thing,
you can't hoard it in a vault. You've got to taste it,
and the more you use it the more you have,
that's the miracle
Sherry Rowe

...

It aint over 'til its over
Yogi Bear

...

Ages of man

How wretched is our lot;
never to possess experience and strength at the same time
King Louis VI

...

On such a world as youth, old age can only gaze with admiration
The plainest girls are pretty with nature's charms
and the dullest buds are at least young
Stephen Leacock

•••

When one surveilles ones aging body
one realises that the only worth having is youth
Anthony Burgess

•••

The best substitute for experience is being sixteen
Raymond Duncan

•••

In our youth we take tests to get into institutions
and in old age we take tests to keep out of them
Alan Bennett

•••

Old people know what it is to have been young and silly,
but the young have never been old and wise
Harold Macmillan

•••

One is only young once
but in some cases that is once too often
Louise de Berniere

•••

It's depressing to see young people miserable,
and depressing to see them happy
Unknown

•••

For most pillars of society,
their second childhood is the only one they experience
Alan Bennett

•••

Some children grow up, others just grow older
Unknown

•••

A child becomes an adult
when he realizes he has the right to be wrong
Unknown

•••

The first half of your life is ruined by your parents
and the second half by your children
Clarence Darrow

•••

Human beings are the only creatures
who allow their children to return home
Unknown

•••

Whoever in middle age
attempts to realize the hopes and wishes of his youth,
deceives himself
Goethe

•••

Middle age ends
when your descendants outnumber your friends
Ogden Nash

•••

Middle age is when your narrow waist
and your broad mind change places
Ben Klitzer

•••

The awful thing about being thirty
is that losing doesn't hurt so much
Jaime Fillol

•••

The trouble with middle age
is there are so many beautiful women
and so little time
John Barrymore

•••

The frightening thing about middle age
is the knowledge that you will grow out of it
Doris Day

•••

One life is an absurdly small allowance
Freya Stark

•••

It is certain we shall not be here for long
and uncertain whether we shall be here even one hour
Blaise Pascal

•••

You should begin to be an old man early
if you want to be an old man long
Cicero

•••

There are three stages in a mans life;
he believes in Santa Clause,
he doesn't believe in Santa Clause,
and he is Santa Clause
Bob Phillips

•••

The older I get the faster I was
Unknown

•••

I am old Sir and now I can say what I like
Mr Bunce

•••

If you were to die soon and could make one last phone call,
who would you call, what would you say,
and why are you waiting
Stephen Levine

•••

If you have 5 minutes left to live,
about the only useful thing you can do
is boil an egg
Unknown

•••

Pity the man who was dealt a winning hand of poker on the Titanic
James Goldsmith

•••

Don't drive faster
than you guardian angel can fly
Unknown

•••

Be a lert, lerts live longer
Unknown

•••

You never get out of this world alive
Hank Williams

•••

Yesterday a drop of semen,
tomorrow a handful of ashes
Marcus Aurelius

•••

I was like a man who had just lost a pawn
and never dreamed this meant checkmate in a few moves
C S Lewis

•••

Whatever happens to you
was prepared from the beginning of time
Marcus Aurelius

•••

Death

Life was a funny thing that happened to me
on the way to the grave
Quentin Crisp

•••

Diversion passes our time
and brings us imperceptibly to our death
Blaise Pascal

•••

Use up your good health
before you're too old to enjoy it
George Bernard Shaw

•••

The only way to keep your health is to eat what you don't want,
drink what you don't like and do what you'd rather not
Mark Twain

•••

In the first stage of seasickness you fear you will die,
In the second stage you fear you won't
Unknown

...

With flu the bottom falls out of your world,
but with Cholera the world falls out of your bottom
Unknown

...

Why preserve life when all must die,
and health is just an ephemeral accident of youth
Homer

...

Time heals and then it kills
Mexican

...

Life is boredom then fear
Whether we use it or not it goes
And leaves what something hidden from us chose
And age and then the only end of age
Philip Larkin

...

Growing old is seldom agreeable
but its better than the alternative
Charley Chan

...

The birth rate and the death rate per person
has never changed throughout history
Unknown

...

One death is a tragedy
but a thousand deaths is a statistic
Joseph Stalin

...

Cigarette smoking is a major cause of statistics
Unknown

...

The last stages of life are a miserable affair,
and yet we are horrified when death comes to put an end to it
Lytton Strachey

...

The House of Lords is like Heaven;
everyone would like to go there, but not yet
Lord Denning

...

Some people wish to achieve immortality
through their works or descendants
I would prefer to achieve it by not dying
Woody Allen

...

I will not renounce the devil on my death bed,
it is no time to make enemies
Voltaire

...

Don't resent growing old,
a great many are denied the privilege
Reinbeck

...

In the long term we are all dead
John Maynard Keynes

...

Live, love work love rest, love all that life can give,
and when you grow too weary to feel joy,
leave life with laughter to some other
Geoffrey Winthrop Young

...

I know I'm going to die but that's allright
You see I've really lived
Cancer patient

...

The Future

Fill a bath with water, put in your fist and pull it out
The size of the hole you leave is how important you were
Paul Terhorst

...

Posterity gives everyone his true value
Tacitus

...

Soon you will have forgotten the world
and the world will have forgotten you
Marcus Aurelius

...

Posterity is as likely to be wrong as anyone else
Heywood Brown

...

Can it matter to you how the tongues of posterity wag
Marcus Aurelius

...

If you get grit in your boots when walking on Haystacks,
treat it with respect, it could be me
A W Wainwright

...

Never make any predictions,
especially about the future
Sam Goldwyn

...

Never think about the future;
it comes soon enough
Unknown

...

The best way to predict the future
is to invent it yourself
Unknown

...

Hope for the best, expect the worst
and take what is offered
Charter Airline Code

...

Who wants to be foretold the weather
Its bad enough when it comes
without the misery of knowing about it in advance
Jerome K Jerome

...

An optimist proclaims we live in the best of all possible worlds
and a pessimist fears this is true
Unknown

•••

Pessimists believe things couldn't be worse;
optimists know they could be
Unknown

•••

Don't worry about the end of the world,
its already tomorrow in Australia
Unknown

•••

My future appears to be behind me
Lyndon Johnson

•••

He who is struck by lightning
has no need to consult the book of omens
Kai Lung

•••

I've set myself up for the future
but my future started sooner than I planned
Gary Mason

•••

I never realised I would be an orphan one day
John Paul Getty

•••

To live is to change
and to be perfect is to change often
Cardinal Newman

•••

Change is the law of life,
and those who look only to the past or the present
are certain to miss the future
J F Kennedy

•••

There is a certain relief from change,
even if it is from bad to worse
Washington Irvine

...

Its like deja vu, all over again
Yogi Bear

...

We are all what we are
and as the years go by, we become more like ourselves
Unknown

...

I do not seek the distant scene,
one step at a time is enough for me
Cardinal Newman

...

Money

The science of life is making money,
the art of life is a sense of humour
Sir Len Hutton

...

Money is my first and last and only love
Armand Hammer

...

The meek shall inherit the earth but not the mineral rights
John Paul Getty

...

In the matter of money all are pigs,
and in the matter of pigs all is money
Unknown

...

It is better to have a permanent income
than to be fascinating
Oscar Wilde

...

In the stock market, every time someone sells another buys
and both think they are astute
William Feather

•••

I buy when other people are selling
John Paul Getty

•••

The first rule of trading stocks and shares is not to panic
Or if you do, to be the first to panic
Anatole Kaletsky

•••

I made my fortune by always selling too soon
My formula is sell, regret and grow rich
Nathan Rothschild

•••

In insurance policies the big print giveth
and the small print taketh away
Unknown

•••

Not everything that counts can be counted,
and not everything that can be counted counts
W B Cameron

•••

Nowadays everyone does everything for money,
and the world will pay for this one day
Fred Zimmerman

•••

When your sponsor comes to justify his costs,
he marks not how you played but if you won or lost
D Prokter

•••

Though a cage be made of gold it is still a prison
Unknown

•••

When a drowning man sank with his treasure bound about him,
did he have the treasure or did the treasure have him?
Unknown

•••

And now for the stuff that makes fools of princes
and princes of fools - money
André Moreau

•••

Among the things that money can't buy,
is what it used to
Max Kaufman

•••

At today's prices
its difficult to make one end meet
Unknown

•••

I know that half my advertising budget is wasted
but I don't know which half
Lord Lever

•••

A bank will only lend you money
if you can prove you don't need it
Unknown

•••

I only rob banks
because that's where the money is
Willy Sutton

•••

If you owe the bank £20,000, you're in trouble
If you owe the bank £20 million, the bank is in trouble
Unknown

•••

There are three kinds of accountants,
those who can count, and those who can't
Eddie George

•••

An auditor is someone
who goes round bayoneting the wounded
Unknown

•••

Administrators are people
who can reduce this year's overspend
from £50m to £100m
Unknown

...

If all the economists in the world were laid end to end
they would still never reach a conclusion
George Bernard Shaw

...

Render unto Visa that which is Visa's
Church Times

...

Those who try to pay their taxes with a smile,
usually find the taxman insists on cash
Unknown

...

There is no convenient time
for childbirth, death or taxes
Margaret Mitchell

...

I always accepted the bribes from both sides,
then I would consider the case on its merits
and return the bribe to the party I found against
English Magistrate in India

...

A racetrack is where the windows clean the people
Unknown

...

It is much more disheartening to have to steal
than to be stolen from
Boris Leomontov

...

No road is safer
than the one just robbed
Mexican

...

If you can count your money
you don't have a billion dollars
John Paul Getty

•••

The really rich are those
who live off the interest from their interest
Unknown

•••

The best way to make a small fortune
is to start off with a big one
Unknown

•••

Misers are not fun to be with,
but they are wonderful ancestors
David Brenner

•••

The landowners of Kent
would gladly give their sons for their country's cause,
but not a square inch of their property
Unknown

•••

If work was all it was cracked up to be,
the rich would have kept it for themselves
Unknown

•••

When the going gets tough
the rich go shopping
Unknown

•••

If one could only get enough of life's luxuries,
one could dispense with necessities
Oscar Wilde

•••

God gives money to the wealthy
because without it they would starve
Mexican

•••

Pity the rich,
in terms of living they are beggars
John Paul Getty

...

The prole suffers physically,
but he is a free man when he is not working
George Orwell

...

No one is rich enough
to be without a neighbour
Unknown

...

It is the privilege of the very poor and the very rich,
to keep their children at home
Laurie Lee

...

Money only buys what is cheap
Unknown

...

Money lost, nothing lost
Courage lost, much lost
Honour lost, more lost
Soul lost, all lost
Dutch

...

He who divides and shares
is left with the best share
Mexican

...

The rich man has a heavy responsibility to serve those less fortunate
and the closer he comes to God,
the more is demanded of him
Gerald Priestman

...

If you have no charity in your heart
you have the worst sort of heart trouble
Bob Hope

...

Poverty

Life is a shit sandwich; the more bread you get to eat
the less shit you have to take
Unknown

•••

Money can't buy happiness
but it takes the edge off being poor
J P Getty

•••

The food of the poor is dreaming
Mexican

•••

Poverty is hereditary,
you get it from your children
Jack Hawkins

•••

Due to financial restraints,
the light at the end of the tunnel will be turned off until further notice
Unknown

•••

When a suit is new it will last 3 years,
when it is old it will last 3 years more,
and when it is patched it will last another 3 years
Mao Tse Tung

•••

The people of Kiloran are not poor
They have no money but that is different
Michael Powell

•••

Honesty

To find an honest man is a true gift from God
Unknown

•••

Bad people do bad things and blame others
Good people do bad things and blame themselves
Unknown

•••

The main thing in life is sincerity,
and if you can fake that you have got it made
George Burns

•••

You can pretend to be serious
but you can't pretend to be witty
Unknown

•••

If you tell the truth you can be sure
you will be found out
Oscar Wilde

•••

If one sticks too rigidly to ones principles
one would hardly see anybody
Unknown

•••

He that hath a secret, should keep it secret
that he has a secret to keep
Thomas Carlyle

•••

When you want to hide something,
put it where everyone can see it
John Coleman

•••

You can't trust a guy who never lost anything
Jake Giddes

•••

Never trust a man who speaks well of everybody
J W Collins

•••

The ultimate judge of your integrity
is the person you see in the mirror
Robert Jahn

•••

He was a good honest man,
you would admire his qualities
but avoid his company
W Somerset Maugham

•••

Give a criminal enough rope
and he will tie up the cashier
Unknown

•••

I try to avoid lying if I possibly can
Alan Clarke MP

•••

He who tells a lie once finds it easier a second time
Thomas Jefferson

•••

If one is libelled, whether you should go to court
or eat toads for breakfast is a pretty close run thing
Unknown

•••

If they stop telling lies about us
we will stop telling the truth about them
Harold Wilson

•••

I do not mind being told a lie,
but not in confidence
Unknown

•••

Never let your morals get in the way of doing what is right
Unknown

•••

These gentleman are my principles
and if you don't like them I'll change them
Unknown

•••

The intellectually honest statesman
changes his opinions rather than his principles
Robert Peel

•••

Our pact with Stalin was not an honest one,
the gap between our ideologies was too wide
Adolph Hitler

...

A verbal agreement isn't worth the paper its written on
Sam Goldwyn

...

Machievelli's prince recognises no morality but sham,
no honour even among thieves, no force but physical force,
no intellectual power but cunning, no disgrace except failure
and no crime but stupidity
Woodrow Wilson

...

Because men are wretched and do not keep their word to you,
you need not keep your word to them
Machievelli

...

Why do men lie about one another
when the plain truth would be bad enough
Unknown

...

We bought the son of a bitch
but he wouldn't stay bought
Standard Oil Company

...

The Standard Oil Company did everything possible
to the Pennsylvania legislature except refine it
Unknown

...

When you pull out the bath plug,
the last thing down the plughole is the scum
Unknown

...

There is not much to choose between men,
they are all a hotchpotch of nobility and baseness
W Somerset Maugham

...

The trouble with human nature is that you are stuck with it
Quentin Crisp

...

Truth

Believe those who seek the truth
but doubt those who find it
Unknown
•••

The pure and simple truth
is rarely pure and never simple
Unknown
•••

Always do right, this will satisfy some people
and astonish the rest
Unknown
•••

Never die for your beliefs
because you might be wrong
Unknown
•••

A thing is not necessarily true
because a man dies for it
Oscar Wilde
•••

For most men the truth is what they feel must be the truth
Justice Holmes
•••

If you repeat a falsehood 1000 times
it becomes truth
Joseph Goebels
•••

An idealist is one who knows that roses smell better than cabbage,
and concludes they will also make better soup
Unknown
•••

If you follow the money,
nine times out of ten it will get you close to the truth
Jake Giddes
•••

We swallow ideas because we like them
and not for their rational content
F A Jones

...

My sources are unreliable
but their information is fascinating
Unknown

...

All those who believe in psychokinesis raise my hand
Unknown

...

Truth is the colour of torquoise,
it varies under different light
Vincent Kofi

...

You can practice until you hit the bulls eye,
or fire your arrow and draw the bulls eye around it
Lionel Blue

...

A fact has scarcely happened 5 minutes
before it is camouflaged by imagination and self interest
Giuseppe di Lampedusa

...

Justice is a contest between two sides playing according to certain rules
If the truth happens to emerge, that's a pure windfall
Ludovic Kennedy

...

A little bit of truth goes a long way
Jake Giddes

...

If you always tell the truth,
you will not have to remember what you said the last time
Sam Rayburn

...

Speak the truth but leave immediately afterwards
Unknown

...

The truth is so important
it must always be accompanied by a body guard of lies
Winston Churchill

...

A new scientific truth does not triumph by convincing its opponents,
but rather when its opponents all die
Max Planck

...

A lie is halfway round the world
before the truth has got its boots on
Unknown

...

God gave Adam the power of speech
and the first thing he did was tell a lie
Unknown

...

You can tell when he's lying when he moves his lips
Harold Wilson

...

The cruellist lies are often told in silence
Robert Louise Stevenson

...

Will someone tell him that denial is not a river in Egypt
Bill Clinton

...

What is the point of lying
when the truth well distributed serves the same purpose
T Wemyss Reid

...

To tell the truth I lied a little
Jake Giddes

...

Never trust the teller trust the tale
D H Lawrence

...

If two extremes are 2 + 2 = 4 and 2 + 2 = 6,
it does not follow that the truth lies in the middle
Peter Skrabanek

...

4 x 6 = 6 x 4
but a blind Venetian is not the same as a Venetian blind
Unknown

•••

New truths begin as heresies
and end as superstitions
T S Huxley

•••

Cynicism is just an unpleasant way of telling the truth
Unknown

•••

Facing up to the truth
is just another form of escapism
Unknown

•••

No one has a monopoly on the truth
Mikel Gorbachov

•••

Knowledge

The first law of hydrodynamics states
that when a body is immersed in water,
the telephone rings
Unknown

•••

If a little learning is a dangerous thing,
think what harm a lot can do
Tom Sharp

•••

There are perilous seas in the world of thought
Bertrand Russell

•••

The port is safety, comfort, hearthstone, supper, warmth, friends
and all that's kind to our mortalities
But in the gale, the port, the land is that ship's direst jeopardy
Herman Melville

...

Even the worst sea is not so terrible in a well appointed ship
Joshua Slocum

...

I know we are ultimately not supposed to know,
but I also know that we are bound to try
The Warden

...

The earth was made round
so that we could not see too far down the road
Karen Blixen

...

All knowledge is but a woven web of guesses
Karl Popper

...

In the high country of the mind one must become adjusted
to the thin air of uncertainty
Robert Pirsig

...

I have approximate answers and possible beliefs,
and different degrees of certainty about different things
But I'm not absolutely sure about anything
and there are many things I don't know anything about;
like whether it means anything to ask why we are here
Richard Feynman

...

Scientists live with doubt and uncertainty
and they make their decisions based on probability
Paul Beeson

...

When the premises are true and the reasoning correct,
the conclusions are only probable
Bertrand Russell

...

Information from the best of men acting with the purist motives,
is sometimes wrong
Thomas Jefferson

•••

The aim of science is not to open a door to infinite wisdom
but to set a limit on infinite error
Berthold Brecht

•••

All analytical statements are tautologies
and all synthetic statements are hypotheses
No universal statement can be proved
and no existential statement can be disproved
Robert Gwyn Macfarlan

•••

If you aren't thoroughly confused
you don't understand the situation
Unknown

•••

For every complex problem there is an easy solution,
and it's wrong
H I Mencken

•••

All generalisations are false
including this one
Fox O'Connor

•••

When there are many remedies
it means there are no cures
Anton Chekov

•••

What's the use of running
when you are on the wrong road
Unknown

•••

An undefined problem
has an infinite number of solutions
Unknown

•••

Even if you are on the right track,
if you just sit there
you will get run over
Unknown

...

Astronomers say the universe is finite,
which is comforting for those
who cannot remember where they leave things
Unknown

...

The supreme achievement of reason
is to realise that there is a limit to reason
Blaise Pascal

...

I want to see a likeness that is deeper
more real than reality
One that is surreal
Pablo Picasso

...

The only watertight way to maintain a case
is never to submit evidence in support of it
A J P Taylor

...

Arguments are extremely vulgar
and everyone in good society
holds exactly the same view
Oscar Wilde

...

The only possible effect you can have on the world
is through unpopular ideas
Viviene Westwood

...

Without competition and collision of opinion,
truth degenerates into dead dogma
John Stuart Mill

...

There are pros and cons for,
and pros and cons against
Henry Cooper

...

If two people agree on absolutely everything
only one of them is doing the thinking
Michael Dukakis

...

Advice is what we ask for
when we already know the answer but wish we didn't
Unknown

...

When two scientists disagree,
they wait for further evidence to decide the issue
When two theologians disagree
there is mutual hatred and an appeal for force
Bertrand Russell

...

In Italy under the Borgias they had war, terror, murder, and bloodshed,
but they produced Michelangelo, Leonardo da Vinci and the Renaissance
In Switzerland they had brotherly love and 500 years of democracy
and produced the cuckoo clock
Graham Greene

...

I hate the Roman called Status Quo
Ask for no security there never was such an animal
Ray Bradbury

...

Men and ideas advance
when the children kill the beliefs of their fathers
Isaiah Berlin

...

If you can see further than others
you are standing on the shoulders of giants
Unknown

...

When faced with the obvious
look elsewhere
Charley Chan

•••

Sometimes the obvious is obvious
Detective Sergeant Lewis

•••

No one knows what he doesn't know,
and the less a man knows
the more sure he is that he knows everything
Joyce Gary

•••

I only know two tunes,
the one is Yankee Doodle Dandy
and the other one isn't
Ulysses Grant

•••

I think the only thing I know
is that I know nothing
Dr John

•••

There are only two kinds of fascinating people,
those who know everything
and those who know nothing
Oscar Wilde

•••

Into the kingdom of knowledge
one can only enter as little child
Francis Bacon

•••

Someone who has never made a fool of himself
will never be wise
Heinrich Heine

•••

The worst pain in the neck
is the know all who is sometimes right
Paul Theroux

...

With art and nature,
shut your mouth and open your eye and ears
C S Lewis

...

When you understand the past,
the present becomes a good deal clearer
John Betjeman

...

The lesson of history
is that people don't learn from history
Unknown

...

Good judgment comes from experience
Experience comes from bad judgment
Unknown

...

It is the mark of an educated man, and proof of his culture,
that in every subject he looks only
for so much proof as its nature permits
and its solution requires
Aristotle

...

To arrive at the core of the matter too quickly
is not to understand with thoroughness
Albert Speer

...

Don't assume
or you will make an ass out of u and me
Unknown

...

If you truly want to understand something
try to change it
Kurt Lewis

...

When you measure things and express them in numbers,
you know something about them
Lord Kelvin

•••

Equations are for eternity
Albert Einstein

•••

98.62 % of statistics
are made up on the spur of the moment
Vic Reeves

•••

Statistics are like a bikini,
they reveal what is interesting but conceal the vital bits
Unknown

•••

Statistics are often used as a drunken man uses a lamp post,
for support rather than illumination
Andrew Lang

•••

If you torture your own data long enough
they will tell you what you want to hear
Unknown

•••

Research is the process of going up alleys to see if they are blind
Unknown

•••

There is only physics,
everything else is stamp collecting
Lord Rutherford

•••

Technology is the name we give to things that don't work yet
Unknown

•••

In God we trust,
but everything we check
Airline Pilot's Creed

•••

Genius is 1% inspiration and 99% perspiration
Thomas Edison

•••

Is it an accident that three men who changed the world,
Marx, Darwin and Freud,
could all have been mistaken for garden gnomes
Unknown

•••

I am so clever that sometimes I don't understand
a single word I'm saying
Oscar Wilde

•••

There are many kinds of stupidity
but cleverness is one of the worst
Thomas Mann

•••

There is nothing so annoying as an argument with someone
who knows what he is talking about
Unknown

•••

Anyone can have common sense
provided they have no imagination
Oscar Wilde

•••

Common sense is the set of prejudices
you learn before the age of eighteen
Albert Einstein

•••

Horse sense is what stops horses betting on people
Raymond Nash

•••

There is a wonderful loneliness in making a discovery
She said how pretty the stars shine,
and he replied that right now
he was the only man who knew why they shone
Richard Feynman

•••

A wise man can tell more from the bottom of a well
than a fool can from a mountain top
Unknown

...

Theologians spend much of their time answering questions
that no one is asking
Unknown

...

People will go to almost any length to avoid thinking
Whitehead

...

The bulk of mankind is as well qualified for flying
as it is for thinking
Jonathon Swift

...

Pioneers are messmakers
and others get to clear up the mess
Robert Pirsig

...

I don't remember a sudden flashing light
but rather a gradual lessening of the darkness
Hans Krebs

...

You cannot jump over a fence in several small leaps
Richard Smith

...

A lot of people mistake their imaginations for their memories
Josh Billings

...

If we are too young our judgment is impaired,
just as when we are too old
Blaise Pascal

...

We say a man dies when his heart stops,
but a man really dies when he loses the power to take in new ideas
Unknown

...

I have more than slept upon it,
I have laid awake on it
Reverend Harding

•••

Even when right,
a scholar can never win an argument with a military man
Pu Yi

•••

To steal ideas from one person is called plagiarism,
to steal from many is called research
Unknown

•••

Research is a race where the fattest survive
Unknown

•••

I have never met a man who was so ignorant
that I could not learn anything from him
Galileo Galilei

•••

Nothing matters much
and very little matters at all
Lord Balfour

•••

He that increaseth knowledge increaseth sorrow
Ecclesiastes

•••

A man standing at the entry of a maze may be nearer the centre
than one who has penetrated far into it
Unknown

•••

The end of all our exploring will be to arrive where we started,
and know the place for the first time
TS Eliot

•••

Education

My 14 months at Magdalene College
proved the most idle and unprofitable of my whole life
Edward Gibbon

...

You can lead a man to college
but you cannot make him think
E Hubbard

...

Education is how a man learns to spell 'experience'
Unknown

...

Bullfight critics ranked in rows,
crowd the enormous plaza full
But only one man really knows
and he's the one who fights the bull
Robert Graves

...

Six honest men taught me all I know,
their names are what, why, when, how where and who
Rudyard Kipling

...

Having no education
I had to use my brains
Bill Shankly

...

It is as easy for a man to have not been to school and know something
as it is for a man to have been to school and know nothing
Tom Jones

...

It is possible to fill the mind with millions of facts
and still be entirely uneducated
Unknown

...

He could talk in 25 languages
but had nothing to say in any of them
Unknown

...

It is the mark of an educated man
to be able to entertain a thought without accepting it
Unknown

...

Education is what survives
when what has been learned has been forgotten
Unknown

...

Education is the ability to listen to almost anything
without losing ones temper
Unknown

...

An Oxford graduate is someone
who can tackle an artichoke with confidence
Unknown

...

You can tell a Balliol man anywhere
but you can't tell him anything
Unknown

...

Education is not the filling of a pail
but the lighting of a fire
W B Yeats

...

If you want to learn something about the world
keep your head empty
Robert Pirsig

...

One should keep an open mind
but distinguish between and open mind and an open sink
P Kurtz

...

I've forgotten what it is I'm trying to remember
Monsieur Argon

...

The English can read and write
and what good has it done them
Chief Kinangui Kikuyu

•••

Some books are to be tasted, others swallowed
and a few thoroughly digested
Unknown

•••

The man who does not read good books
has no advantage over the man who cannot read
Mark Twain

•••

Philosophy books have small print, big words and no sales
Alfred Hitchcock

•••

I have found rest nowhere
except in a corner with a book
Thomas a Kempis

•••

If the universities were just for teaching,
they would still be teaching that the world is flat
Unknown

•••

The scholarship boys were cynically crammed with knowledge
like a goose is crammed for Christmas
George Orwell

•••

Jerediah Buxton could calculate in 90 seconds
how many barley corns stretched 8 miles
When taken to the theatre to see Richard III,
he spent his time counting the words spoken by David Garrick
Unknown

•••

Remember first at school means last in life
Unknown

•••

After a PhD, the student is pronounced completely full,
and after this, no new ideas can be imparted to him
Stephen Leacock

•••

The pupils who seemed the laziest
are eminent now in business and public life
whilst the prize boys are only able to earn the wages of a clerk
Stephen Leacock

•••

To ensure the greatest efficiency of the dart,
the harpooneers of this world
must start to their feet from out of idleness
and not from out of toil
Herman Melville

•••

There is only one reason for going to university
and that is to learn to get drunk like a gentleman
David Montague

•••

Wittenburg university was pre eminent for its beer drinking,
Marburg for the number of duels fought,
and Leipzig for its licentiousness
Gordon Craig

•••

A war can do what 30 years at university might have done
Unknown

•••

One should always pass on advice,
its the only thing its good for
Oscar Wilde

•••

I usually give people the advice they want,
otherwise they take no notice
James Callaghan

•••

The wise man pays head to current opinion
before deciding for himself
Unknown

•••

Even a blind hog can find an acorn once in a while
Lyndon Johnson

•••

All professors do is make a lot of noise
and ask for money
David Weatherall

•••

Professors whores and ballet dancers
can all be bought with money
Ernst August

•••

In a free society the notion that authority is entitled to reverence
is the most subversive of all
Arthur Schlesinger

•••

Authority is entitled to the respect it earns
and not one whet more
Lord Acton

•••

Have no respect for authority,
but ask yourself is this reasonable
Richard Feynman

•••

If they give you ruled paper
write the other way
Juan Jiminez

•••

The Royal Society was like the Pacific Palola worm;
it lost every faculty save that of reproduction,
and all the fellows did was elect other fellows
Unknown

•••

When I got into the Arista I discovered that all they wanted to talk about
was who else should be allowed into the Arista
Richard Feynman

•••

What am I doing here being tried by twelve people
who aren't clever enough to avoid doing jury service
Unknown

•••

Insanity

It is not yet settled whether madness is the loftiest intelligence
Edgar Allan Poe

...

Our greatest blessings come by way of madness
Socrates

...

Blake was undoubtedly mad , but his madness was
infinitely more interesting than Sir Walter Scott's sanity
William Wordsworth

...

We need a few madmen around these days,
after all look where the sane ones have landed us
Bertrand Russell

...

All men of genius are mad
but not all sane people are idiots
Samuel Butler

...

There is only one difference between a madman and me;
I am not mad
Salvador Dali

...

If you cling to the truth even against the whole world
you are not mad
Sanity is not statistical
George Orwell

...

They said I was mad and I said they were mad,
and my God, they out voted me
Unknown

...

Of doctor, poet, musician and madman,
we each have a trace
Mexican

...

Who in the rainbow can draw the line between orange and violet
So with sanity and insanity
Herman Melville

•••

The boundary between the throne and the madhouse
is a slender one
Unknown

•••

The purpose of life is to stay alive
but only a madman would ask why
Robert Pirsig

•••

From little sleep and too much reading
his brain dried up and he lost his wits
Cervantes

•••

Stupidity has saved many a man from madness
Michael Powell

•••

Reality is over rated, once you have seen one bit of it
you've seen it all
Oscar Wilde

•••

Its not your enemies who condemn you to solitude
but your friends
Milan Kundera

•••

Facing up to one's problems is only another form of escapism
Richard Needham

•••

There is no more despicable thing
than the man who flees from his demons
Joseph Conrad

•••

He that flees may know what he flees from
but not what he seeks
Montaigne

•••

Whatever you turn your back on
gets you in the end
Michael Mayer

•••

If you are paranoid it does not mean
that someone has not got it in for you
Unknown

•••

A symptom of approaching nervous breakdown
is the belief that one's work is terribly important
Bertrand Russell

•••

Fanatics can not change their mind
and will not change the subject
Winston Churchill

•••

A well balanced man is one with a chip on each shoulder
Unknown

•••

Be generous and liberal in your attitude to irrational men
for you have reason and they have none
Marcus Aurelius

•••

When you are in the shadow of insanity,
the appearance of another mind
that thinks and talks like you
is something close to a blessed event
Robert Pirsig

•••

Hollywood is where they place you under contract
instead of observation
Unknown

•••

Neurotics build castles in the air,
psychotics live in them and psychiatrists collect the rent
J Lawrence

•••

Anyone who consults a psychiatrist
needs to have his head examined
Sam Goldwyn

...

Religion

It is easier to fight for ones religious principles
than to live up to them
Unknown

...

One man thinks it is lawful to eat pork but not beef,
another beef but not pork,
The result of this difference of opinion is usually bloodshed
Bertrand Russell

...

I am not a pillar of the church but more a flying buttress
I support the church from the outside
Churchill

...

All sensible men have the same religion
Benjamin Disraeli

...

Protestants like to be good and have invented theology
in order to keep themselves so
Catholics like to be bad and have invented theology
to keep their neighbours good
Bertrand Russell

...

The Catholic church is for saints and sinners,
for respectable people the Anglican church will do
Oscar Wilde

...

It doesn't matter if you don't believe in transubstantiation,
but you must either kneel or get out of the church
Unknown

...

The horror of the Christian universe
is that it has no door marked 'exit'
C S Lewis

•••

To the repentant thief, Jesus declares
you are in Paradise right now
Peter Mattiesson

•••

A young atheist must guard his faith carefully,
dangers lie in wait for him on every side
C S Lewis

•••

If I must live without God
then so must you
Sigmund Freud

•••

Christians are wrong
but all the rest are bores
Roland

•••

The final proof of God's omnipotence
is that he doesn't have to exist in order to save mankind
Peter de Vries

•••

An omnipotent God could create such a great rock
that even He could not lift it
Unknown

•••

WH Auden didn't love God
He just fancied him
Graham Greene

•••

It is a privilege to be mocked for God
Lord Longford

•••

Faith may vanish
but the need for faith remains the same
Kabril Gibran

•••

Faith is believing something you know is not true
Paul Theroux

•••

The higher the intelligence the more the faith
and the less credulity
Herman Melville

•••

The things I assert most vigorously
are those I resisted long and accepted late
C S Lewis

•••

There is nothing worth living for,
save Christian architecture and a boat
Augustus Pugin

•••

The sense of futility is the subtlest weapon of the devil
Unknown

•••

When we talk to God it is called prayer,
when God talks to us it is called schizophrenia
Unknown

•••

I have never seen God but I believe I have heard Him
C S Lewis

•••

When the gods wish to punish us
they answer our prayers
Oscar Wilde

•••

If God answered petitionary prayers,
the laws of nature would be subverted
and the world would become completely unpredictable
C S Lewis

•••

Miracles have causalities which can be traced back to the origin of time,
and which predate any prayer to God to intervene miraculously
Malcolm Lowry

•••

•••

Prayer does not change God,
it changes him who prays
Soren Kierkergaard

•••

Pray not to be spared suffering
but for the strength to bear it
Unknown

•••

Oh Lord we pray thee not that wrecks should happen,
but if they do, thou wilt guide them to the coast of Cornwall
for the benefit of the poor inhabitants
Daphne du Maurier

•••

Oh Lord if it be thy will,
help us to rise above the clouds and grant us a safe journey
Archbishop's pilot

•••

Physics without God
would be a dull enquiry into certain meaningless phenomena
Canon Pusey

•••

Whenever you hear the bible quoted
its usually the devil doing the quoting
Lady Despard's butler

•••

Most people in sight of the spiritual mountains never enter them,
but are content to listen to others who have been there,
and thus avoid the hardships
Robert Pirsig

•••

Too many Christians want to reach the Promised Land
without going through the wilderness
Unknown

•••

The line between good and evil does not run between people
but through them
Unknown

•••

The only difference between a sinner and a saint
is that one has found forgiveness
and the other one aint
Bill Clinton

•••

We mortals are such as God made us
and some are much worse
Henry Fielding

•••

I've seldom met a person more endowed with vices
and thank God I know it
Leo Tolstoy

•••

In hell people sat round a pot of soup
but their spoons were so long they could not eat
Heaven was the same scene
but everyone used their long spoons to feed one another
Rabbi Jonathan Romain

•••

The only form of hell
would be to contemplate of the gifts we have wasted
Wim van Leer

•••

Hell is a jungle clearing
where a man is forced to read Dickens to a lunatic
over and over again
Evelyn Waugh

•••

If you get to be famous you go straight to Hell
Zen Master

•••

To everyone is given the keys of the gates of Heaven
The same keys fit the gates of Hell
Buddhist

•••

It would be nice to see Heaven
before Capability Brown has chance to improve it
Unknown

•••

People who worry about the next world
usually make themselves a bloody nuisance in this one
Lady Despard's butler

...

If you must choose between two evils
pick the one you've never tried before
Unknown

...

Children must be taught the difference
between good and evil
or they will just end up as clever devils
Rhodes Boyson

...